Myths about missions

To Helen

Myths about missions

A challenge to face the truth
Horace L Fenton

Inter-Varsity Press

Copyright © 1973 by
Inter-Varsity Christian Fellowship, USA
INTER-VARSITY PRESS
Inter-Varsity Fellowship
39 Bedford Square, London WC1B 3EY
First British edition 1974

ISBN 0 85110 375 8
Printed in England by
Arrowsmith Ltd

CONTENTS

PUBLISHERS' NOTE:

Dr Fenton is a North American with leadership responsibilities in the Latin America Mission. His book reflects his background, and some of his emphases might be slightly different were he writing, say, in Britain. But he challenges effectively the traditional missionary thinking of many Christians throughout the Western world. It is a challenge which needs to be heard and heeded.

PREFACE

The conviction that much of our missionary thinking is based on myths, rather than on biblical truth, had been with me for a long time. The invitation from President Vernon Grounds and Professor Ralph Covell to deliver a series of mission lectures at the Conservative Baptist Theological Seminary in Denver, Colorado, crystallized my desire to share my concern about the mixture of myth and Scripture with students and with other thinking Christians.

Mr. David Howard, my friend and erstwhile colleague in the work in Latin America and currently Missions Director of the Inter-Varsity Christian Fellowship, encouraged me in the preparation of the manuscript. I owe much to him and to some of my other co-workers in the Latin America Mission

—men like the late R. Kenneth Strachan, W. Dayton Roberts and Ruben Lores, who by their devotion to Christ and by their freedom in him to evaluate and to criticize our traditional missionary thinking have stimulated my mind and deepened my commitment to the gospel.

Dr. Paul Rees, whose prophetic voice and pen have meant so much to the church of Christ and the cause of missions, wrote a series of editorials in World Vision Magazine some years ago on the subject of myths which have crowded into our missionary thinking. The precision of his thought and the careful articulation of his convictions have been of great benefit to me.

Miss Molly Fahringer, who as my secretary has helped me so much in all of my work in the Latin America Mission, has been of immense help in the preparation of this manuscript. I am very grateful.

To all who have assisted me in coming to a more truly biblical view of missions, I express my thanks. If I can be of help to others in the same way, I shall feel I have in some small sense paid part of the debt I owe to so many who have corrected my thinking and enriched my life.

Horace L. Fenton, Jr.
Bogota, New Jersey

THE MYTHOLOGY OF MISSIONS

Myths about missions? The two things just don't go together in the minds of most Christians. To them, missions are the fulfillment of the Great Commission, which they memorized in childhood. Bible verses, coupled with missionary reports—and missionary slides, including the inevitable sunset scene!—are missions to them.

But if you have had contact with many evangelical churches and their missionary conferences, you may have noticed that we Christians have unwittingly mixed a good many mythical elements with our missionary convictions. The result of that mixture is that our missionary motivations and our missionary methods are often sub-biblical. We have become the victims of a full-blown mythology that we ourselves have created and believed, and the consequences are often disastrous.

If this be true (and I hope to demonstrate its truth in the remainder of this book), a tremendous job of missionary re-education needs to be done at the grass-roots level. It is not enough to criticize the churches or to try to fix the blame for the confused state of their thinking about missions. Instead, the myths need to be identified and their unscriptural content exposed.

Where did these myths come from? Who propagated them? We all bear a share of the blame. Missions and missionaries, meaning to be honest in the presentation of the truth concerning God's work in the world, have often unwittingly given a highly subjective picture of that which they have seen and experienced. Moreover, those at home have ordinarily heard only one side of the missionary story. You may have listened to many missionaries tell of their work, but how many national Christians from other lands have been given a chance to tell you how they view the situation?

Bishop Stephen Neill puts the matter very bluntly when he says, "Christian history has been written far too much from the side of the operators, and far too little from that of the victims.... We know fairly well what it feels like to be a missionary; we know far less of what it feels like to be the object of the missionary's attentions."[1]

Pastors have repeated what they have heard missionaries or other pastors say, without subjecting these statements to the judgment of Scripture or to the scrutiny of history. Lay people who love the Lord and long for the evangelization of the world have implicitly believed and repeated what they have been told about missions, often without perceiving that what they are passing on is a strange mixture of myth and biblical truth.

Failure to Keep Pace

Frequently, our readiness to believe and propagate myths about missions arises from our failure to keep pace with history. Nothing goes out of date so quickly today as reports on missionary work! If you hear a missionary message today that could have been given twenty-five years ago, something is wrong. Either the reporter is out of touch with reality, or he is deliberately choosing not to give you the whole picture.

To be sure, the missionary's basic message remains unchanged, but its context has changed so rapidly—and so radically—in recent years that many of us, too little aware of how different the situation is today, are in grave danger of disseminating myths when we really mean to be giving an honest report.

Norman Horner states, "The Protestant missionary enterprise has undergone more radical changes in the last fifteen years than in the previous century."[2] Yet missionary speakers often give the impression that nothing has changed. We thereby provide fertile ground in which myths about missions can grow and flourish. Mistaken concepts of missions are repeated, believed, perpetuated. We sound the same old themes, tell the same old stories, show the same sympathy-eliciting slides and fail to recognize that we thus reinforce ideas 11 which, if they were ever true, are long since outdated.

Picture yourself as an international student from a large city in Africa—Nairobi, Kampala, Johannesburg. You lived in a modern dormitory at the university during your undergraduate days. You shopped in large department stores. Then, while studying in North America, you attend a church missionary conference with some Christian friends. There in the display area is a simulated grass hut, made with chicken wire covered with brown crepe paper. Under the crepe paper palm tree rests—in its pot—an African violet. The missionary tells how the native women all start wearing blouses once they are converted (he shows pictures). How do you feel about this representation of your continent?

The average church member has been discouraged from questioning the things he hears from the pulpit, and so the opinions of missionaries and pastors concerning the task of world evangelization are often given the same validity as the proclamation of God's unchanging truth.

No wonder a mythology has grown up around missions! No wonder many of the myths dealt with in this book have been given the status of gospel truth!

At best, these myths are harmless little fables which the church may in time outgrow, as it becomes more mature. At worst, they are misconceptions, false motivations and distortions of the truth that hamper the work of Christ and that often compromise the whole missionary enterprise.

Myths Are Dangerous

If I have not overstated the potential danger of these false ideas, they ought not to be dismissed lightly or to be ignored, in the hope that they will somehow go away in due time. Humanly speaking, the future of the missionary effort depends on our constantly bringing all our missionary concepts and convictions under the judgment of Scripture. We must then be willing to reject ruthlessly that which does not conform to biblical standards, and that which the experience of the years or the rapid changes in our own time have proven to be invalid.

I stress the word *ruthlessly*. Sir Arthur Quiller-Couch, renowned authority on English literature, used to warn his students against the overblown, overornamented style which often characterized their writings, nourished by their love of high-sounding phrases. His dramatic way of expressing the warning was by saying, "Murder your darlings!"—meaning that they should ruthlessly eliminate those pet phrases which added nothing to their message and indeed diminished its impact.

Some of the myths which have gathered around the missionary enterprise have become "darlings" to us in the church of Christ. They have been held so long and cherished so dearly that we have equated them with gospel truth and, as a result, to question their validity seems almost heretical. But if in the light of Scripture these concepts prove to be myths rather than God's truth, they need to be murdered, and that without delay.

Most of us are conformists by nature, and as we grow older we find it harder and harder to change 13 either our actions or the concepts that lie behind them. Increasingly, we tend to accept as truths those things which we have heard repeatedly or read in the proper places, and we cling to these concepts tenaciously, changing our thinking only with great reluctance. We become like those preachers who are "forever baptizing the status quo."[3]

In the realm of thought as well as of action our theme song often seems to be "Come weal or come woe, my status is quo." We resist change everywhere, and nowhere more than in the realm of long-cherished ideas. Result: We think wrongly and often unbiblically. We become the victims of our own myths. All unconsciously, we have married our myths to God's truth, and it is time we put asunder what man has joined together.

In one sense this is the work of Satan, as is any opposition to the spread of the gospel. But having said that, we cannot thereby escape our responsibility for the persistence and the proliferation of these myths.

This book represents a limited attempt to identify some of the myths which have crept into our missionary thinking, by showing how far short of God's revealed truth these concepts fall and how deadly is their effect if they are allowed to go unchallenged. Perhaps, if error is thus exposed, we shall be able to understand more fully the true purposes of God and our part in the divine plan for carrying them out.

THE MYTH
OF THE LIMITED CALL:
THE YOUNG ELITE

Through the years the idea has somehow got abroad that the missionary call is limited to a relatively small group of people who, by their special gifts or their special relationship to the Lord, are honored by an invitation from God to become members of the spiritual elite that we call "missionaries."

This is one of the myths that have gathered around the cause of missions in our time. By a misreading of the Scripture and by a consequent misunderstanding of the purposes of God down through the years, we have given a false representation of the missionary call to many generations of Christians. The effects of such misinformation on individual lives and on the missionary enterprise are far-reaching indeed.

You cannot be expected, however, to recognize the myth or to see its dangers when it is described in such general terms. Therefore, let us look at some of the ways in which this false teaching has manifested itself. We will consider two in this chapter and two in the next.

Going, Giving, Praying

First, the idea of the limited call has been popularized as a slogan. I saw it first as a child in the junior department of my home Sunday school. The room in which we met was decorated with religious mottos which must have made some impression on our childish minds; I can still remember them after all these years. One of them said, "Expect great things from God; attempt great things for God." Another—the one which especially concerns us here—said, "Some can go; most can give; all can pray."

I thought this was great—a helpful expression of a spiritual truth. I continued to feel that way about it long after I had left the junior department, and I venture to believe that it may have been the basis of more than one sermon that I gave in the early days of my ministry. I could almost see the concentric circles involved: the small group in the center —those who go; the slightly larger circle—those who give; the largest circle—those who pray.

It sounds so pious! It seems to be saying, "Everybody is involved, but in different ways, and each man can somehow find his place." How comforting! There is an element of truth in all this, of course—enough truth so that we find ourselves quoting the statement as though it were really a part of biblical revelation. But it isn't! On closer examination, we see that this beautiful slogan is so patently a distortion of the truth as to be a myth, and a deadly one at that.

The issue here is, Who are to be involved in the missionary enterprise and what form is their involvement to take? Let's look at this teaching. It begins by saying, "Some can go." This really implies the concept of a missionary elite—a specially favored, highly talented, relatively small group who are God's little band for getting the world evangelized. It sounds plausible, because it corresponds to so much that we have heard and seen.

God does seem to call a limited number to go long distances and to cross geographic and cultural frontiers with the message of the gospel. In a unique sense, he lays upon some of his servants a special burden for the unreached multitudes, particularly in those lands where there has been little or no opportunity to know the gospel in its fullness and power.

But the error in all this comes when we begin to believe that the "going" that God wants done is confined to this little group and is characterized chiefly by traveling long distances over much salt water to many strange lands. Involved here is a distortion of the whole missionary concept, which may well have encouraged wrong thinking by several generations of Christians.

The Elite

For one thing, it has often caused the church to 17

make an undue fuss over this elite group, because they are relatively few in number, because they seem to be making great sacrifices, and because those who are left behind inevitably feel a sense of guilt about not going themselves. And so the church has alternately praised and felt sorry for this little band—the "some" who could go.

In moments inspired by a sense of guilt or by a desire for greater personal dedication, the rest of us promise to pray for them and to pay for them. None of these reactions is necessarily wrong or unworthy in itself, but by exaggerating the role of those who travel great distances and go to strange places, we soon tend to underestimate the importance of the divine call to *all* Christians.

This view causes us to place an unduly geographical emphasis on missions. Location tends to become more important than vocation, and we thereby reverse the biblical priorities. To be sure, the Bible takes notice of geography, but it doesn't make one place more important than another. God's emphasis is on the world, and this means the world close at hand as well as the world far away, the world all too familiar as well as the world exotic. Moreover, in Acts 1:8 it is apparent that, while places are named, their order is not necessarily sequential or climactic.

Some are to go to each of these places, and it would seem that there ought to be equal honor and an equally high title for those who serve Jesus Christ because they know themselves to be sent to Jerusalem, with all its hatred for our Lord and his gospel, as for those who go to the ends of the earth.

Another strange consequence of this idea that only a few can go and that going necessarily involves considerable distance is that in the church we have tended to give an unbiblical glamour to that which is unknown and far off. A friend of mine left a fine position in the business world a few years ago to become superintendent of a mission situated in the heart of a city that had been devastated by riots. He has given himself unstintingly to the needs of the people of that city and has seen a real measure of the Lord's blessing upon his efforts. Yet he confessed to me a great disappointment over the attitude of supposedly dedicated Christians in a thriving suburban church located on the outskirts of that city.

This church prides itself on its missionary-mindedness and boasts of the size of its missions budget and of the length of its missionary roll. When my friend appealed to the young people of the church to come help him reach the ghetto young people for Christ, he found them willing and eager—but their Christian parents refused to let them go! The inner city was too dangerous for their children, they said. They dared not allow them to go there.

Yet these same parents would have felt proud if their children had been called to the heart of Africa and would have been perfectly willing to trust the Lord to protect them against the dangers they might encounter there. For all their protestations of missionary interest, these parents had only a very limited idea of what missionary work is all about.

19

Because we have given the idea that missions is the work of a small group, we have forgotten that the Bible teaches that each Christian is to put himself at the disposal of his Lord and that this principle is much more basic than the question of where he is to go. When our Lord Jesus, on the first Easter evening, announced to his disciples his basic plan ("So send I you"), he must have left many unanswered questions in their minds.

I can picture one of them saying, "Lord, where are you going to send us?" To which the Lord's reply might have been, "The question of your location is secondary and can be dealt with later. The basic thing for you to understand right now is that, because you are mine, I am sending you just as the Father sent me."

Another disciple might well have asked, "Lord, what are we going to do?" And a similar reply would have come back, "You'll learn that in good time. The important thing now is to remember that, as a disciple of mine, you are to be a sent one, a missionary."

You see, the way we have limited the missionary call has caused us to fail to understand that the going for Christ is only one part of being his disciple. As a result, we have missed the truth of which Trueblood has written: "Christians do not merely send missionaries, they are missionaries."[1]

Across the Street

Having accepted the idea that only some can go, we have put into missions an element of phoniness which the Scriptures would reject and which young people in our day will have no part of. Very frequently, when I go to a church for a missionary conference, one of the older members comes to me and says, "Oh, Mr. Fenton, we're praying that many of our young people will hear the missionary call this week."

I appreciate the concern thus expressed, but I find myself wanting to say, "Well, I'm praying that *you'll* hear the missionary call this week! Your age has nothing to do with the matter! If you are a Christian, God wants to send you somewhere, and the young people will be much more likely to respond to the call of Christ when they see their parents and other adults going wherever the Lord sends them. He wants to send every one of his disciples; some of them will be sent across the street, and some across the world, but *all* of them will be sent somewhere."

When will we ever get onto this basic biblical truth? I do not deny that there is a special sense in which some may be called to cross geographic and cultural frontiers for Christ, but I insist that the Bible knows nothing of the narrow, limited concept that we have given to missionary work. Of course, it is true that some of God's servants are called to strange places and to pioneer areas. It is also true that, relatively speaking, this is a small group (although I suspect that God never meant it to be as small as it has been down through the ages). But the clear teaching of Scripture is that *all* of God's children are intended to go with the gospel— to go somewhere for Jesus' sake and because he has sent them.[2]

21

I like Dr. John Howard Yoder's insistence that in the Great Commission the imperative is not to "go" but to "make disciples."[3] This respected Mennonite theologian claims that a much better translation of this familiar verse would be, "As you go, preach," and he makes out a good case for this emphasis. It is as though the Lord took it for granted that everyone would go somewhere, and consequently he put his emphasis not on our going but on the fact that, as we go, every one of us is meant to be a witness for Christ.

It is our relationship to him, through faith and by grace, that makes us not only candidates for missionary service but in a very real sense conscripts for that service. If this be true, and I am sure that it is, then we have told less than half the truth with our insistence that "some can go." The great awakening that has come to the church of Christ in Latin America in recent years has in part been due to a rediscovery of the scriptural emphasis that, in the plan and purpose of God, *all* are meant to go.

Indeed, this is the kind of thing that gives fresh hope to the cause of missions, as Trueblood points out when he says, "if the church were limited to a shrinking number of professionals, there might be reason for discouragement, but there is immense hope in the scattering of committed Christians as they pursue their secular occupations."[4]

That same discovery is being made, thank God, in some churches here in the homeland. As a result, the church is seen not as a building, but as a body of Christians who are gathered together on Sunday for worship, then scattered for service throughout the rest of the week, as its members go to the places where God sends them.

The men go back to business on Monday morning not just because this is the way they earn their living, but because Christ sends them there. They are his missionaries to the business world. The women of the church go to their tasks in the home, in the neighborhood or in the world of commerce, not merely because this is the nature of their lives, but because they are sent by Christ to these places. They have discovered their mission fields. And the young people go back to their schools and colleges, not just because it is a good thing to get an education, but because this is where they are called to be the servants of God.

The true measure of the missionary-mindedness of a church is not its missionary budget, not the number of people it supports abroad, but the proportion of its own members who recognize that be-because they are saved by Christ they are meant to be sent by Christ.

Who Is Exempt?

By the same token, the seemingly innocent statement, "Most can give," has undoubtedly done its share of harm in the missionary enterprise. It seems to be a sort of kindly recognition that some people cannot give. Such an emphasis appears, on the surface, to have much to commend it; it looks like a sympathetic recognition that some people are too poor to give and therefore ought not to be forced to do so, while the majority who can give ought to provide the support for the Lord's work.   **23**

Obviously, there is some truth here, also. But the way it is usually cited gives an emphasis that falls far short of a scriptural position. The New Testament states with approval the example of those who gave out of their poverty. And it insists that all of us have been given some gift by God and therefore have something to return to him by way of service for him and for our fellow men. God's gifts do not always come in the form of finances, to be sure, but what we have from him is meant to be shared so that the needs of others may be met.

Particularly in North America, where so many of us Christians are so well off, it seems almost heresy to propagate the idea that some cannot give. In the average white Anglo-Saxon Protestant church there is scarcely anyone who can legitimately be excused.

Recently I was preaching in a missionary conference on 2 Corinthians 9:8, 11, which reads in the New English Bible: "And it is in God's power to provide you richly with every good gift; thus you will have ample means in yourselves to meet each and every situation, with enough and to spare for every good cause. . . . You will always be rich enough to be generous."

In the congregation were a middle-aged Korean man and his son, an anesthesiologist who recently had begun practice in the States. The father heads up a Christian social service work among the needy children of Korea. He understands no English, but he followed the reading of the above verses in his Bible as I preached, and his son occasionally interpreted to him the nature of my comments.

Afterwards the older man said to me, "Second Corinthians 9:8 is a good verse for the Christians in America!" And I knew what he meant. The people in that church were wealthy, in his eyes. In a country like this, to allow some Christians to escape from the privilege of giving for the cause of Christ is no service to them. And it is surely no service to the cause of Christ. I earnestly believe that many a Christian who could give for the spread of the gospel is excusing himself from doing so on the basis of the myth which says that only a certain part of the church is expected to give.

Optional Sharing

Actually, people who hide behind an excuse like this one are usually not the poorest of the believers, but those who are well above the poverty level and who want to find a way to escape sharing with Christ and with needy humanity. In the great churches of our own land this is likewise true. The large givers there are often not the rich; rather, they are those with limited means who are already seemingly stretched to the limit of their giving, but who refuse to excuse themselves from engaging further in this great Christian responsibility and privilege. Some deliberately adopt a more modest life style in order to make a large missions pledge.

My experience with Christians in Latin America leads me to believe that the poor are often the most generous. They do not hide behind the excuse that only "most can give"; they see giving as a normal part of their Christian experience. Undernourished themselves, they share food with those who have

25

less; hard put financially, they always seem to find some way of supporting the work of the Lord and of helping those less fortunate than themselves.

Our North American slogans have fortunately not penetrated some of these younger churches. As a result, new believers feel that giving is not an option but a privilege, and one to be engaged in no matter how pitifully small their resources are.

Prayer Is Costly

Of course, no one can quarrel with the part of the slogan that reminds us that "all can pray." On the other hand, if some believers realized how costly true prayer is, they might want to delegate this privilege also to a smaller group, excusing themselves from the stern demands of earnest intercession.

We need to remember that the prayers of God's people help to produce fruitfulness in the labors of those who are devoting their full time to the spread of the gospel. I experience the reality of this power in my own life, as others pray for me, even when I cannot understand its rationale. We do God's people and God's work a real favor when we teach them to involve themselves meaningfully in prayer. But prayer of this sort is not play; it is hard work, and just as demanding in its own way as going or giving. Indeed, it is a form of both going and giving.

What we have been saying here is that some of our slogans become myths, and that the myths are often sub-Christian. What sounds like lovely, pious sentiment may in reality be an attempt to settle for considerably less than the biblical ideal.

If we understand the Scriptures correctly, what we ought to be saying to ourselves and to all believers is that *all* can go—and therefore should; *all* can give—and are therefore under an obligation to do so; *all* can pray—and this is an essential accompaniment of the going and the giving, but no substitute for either one of them.

When the church of Jesus Christ comes to see that each of us as a believer is called to all three of these ministries, then an impetus will be given to the worldwide spread of the gospel such as will please the heart of God and bless the outreach of his church.

Only the Young

Second, *the call has been limited to a certain age group.* The counter culture thought it had invented a new slogan a few years ago when it said, "Don't trust anyone over thirty!" Actually, mission boards have been propagating that idea for years, as far as candidates are concerned. For too long a time we managed to communicate to the Christian church the idea that the missionary call is for people under thirty years of age.

Fortunately, that stress is not heard quite so frequently in our circles today, but the myth lingers on and continues to do its deadly work, serving to exclude from the service of Christ great numbers of people who might be very useful for him. Besides, this emphasis has often served to provide an excuse for halfhearted Christians who are eagerly looking for ways in which to escape their missionary responsibility.

27

Of course, there are some valid reasons for the stress on responding to the call at an early age. The advantages of getting to the field as a young adult are fairly obvious. Children and young people ordinarily have less difficulty in adapting to a new culture than do their elders. Moreover, younger people are thought to have greater facility in learning a new language. (Linguists now dispute this point, however, and can cite much evidence which indicates that age is not so great a factor in language learning as we once thought.)

Unquestionably, younger people ordinarily tend to be freer of cares, concerns and heavy responsibilities, and in this sense they may be able to adjust to new circumstances more readily and to learn to think in a foreign language more quickly; but there is no "great divide" at the age of thirty, and many an older person has learned a strange tongue better than some who were his junior by many years.

Without denying the advantages of youth, missions have been learning in recent years that the chronological age of a candidate is not so significant as many other factors. There is clear evidence, as a result of advanced psychological research, that most people have a greater capacity for continued growth and hence for usefulness than we previously recognized, and that this capacity does not disappear at any particular age.

An older person who is highly motivated may do much better in learning a language, for example, or in adapting to the ways of a strange culture than a younger person who has not fully thought through his reasons for being in the new situation.

Moreover, we have long since seen, in missionary circles, that in the service of Christ there is no substitute for maturity, and that maturity comes chiefly through time and experience. Many of us have learned to thank God that some of our present-day candidates are coming to us with a greater wealth of experience and understanding than was the case with their younger predecessors. This has been possible only because the age level of new missionaries is today higher than it used to be.

If the call of Christ is as universal as we have been insisting here, then obviously age has relatively little to do with it. Other factors are much more important than this one. Like any other mission executive, I could cite almost innumerable examples of older people who have come to us in recent years and who have discovered that God was opening up to them a whole new chapter in their lives, for which he had wonderfully fitted them by the years and the experience that had gone before.

I think of one couple who were in their fifties when they arrived on the field and who have had a marvelously fruitful ministry. To have turned them down, as we would formerly have done, on the basis that they had passed the magic age of thirty (and were therefore presumably on the sunset slope of life!) would have been tragedy— tragedy because their own potential in the service of Christ would have been unrealized, and tragedy because the work of Christ in some area of the world would have been less effective without them. **29**

Almost all of us have at one time or another accepted uncritically the myth that a person's usefulness for God begins to diminish at a certain age, and that therefore there is no hope of active missionary service for those who begin their careers in middle life. We have believed an untruth, and it is time to set our own thinking straight and then to help our fellow Christians see how utterly untrustworthy is this myth.

But this "myth of the limited call" takes other forms as well, and we shall have a look at some of them in the following chapter.

3

THE MYTH
OF THE LIMITED CALL:
PERMANENT AND
TRADITIONAL

Like a deadly virus which keeps breaking out in new diseases, the myth of the limited call manifests itself in a wide diversity of ways. All these manifestations have in common a tendency to restrict missionary service to a select few, whereas God wants to send all of his children somewhere with the gospel of Christ. The missionary call is universal, and we do well to note the false concepts which tend to limit that call. Here are two more aspects of the myth we are considering:

Life Sentence?
First, *a missionary call is thought to be for life.* This concept is widely accepted, and as a result we have given potential candidates the impression that anyone who is not ready to make a lifelong   31

commitment is somehow unworthy of missionary appointment, and that anyone who leaves the "mission field" before age 65 is a quitter, going back to the homeland to settle for something less than God's best.

In a sense, of course, discipleship is always for life. But location is something else! We do not expect a pastor to stay in the same church all his life, nor do we charge him with spiritual shortcoming if he goes from one field of service to another. Surely we do not believe that service in some lightly populated area is necessarily more virtuous than service in suburbia or in a crowded city. And surely a person who goes from one to the other does not thereby prove himself a success or a failure in the work of Christ!

It is conceivable that on occasion God would want a man in Africa for a limited number of years, then bring him back to North America for the rest of his earthly life to share with Christians here what he learned of the Lord and from his church in a faraway land. In such a case, the ministry in North America would not represent any spiritual demotion, since it was in the will of God.

Moreover, we are learning that the missionary enterprise has to be much more flexible than we used to allow it to be. Mobility will have to become our keynote if the work is to be carried out effectively and in the will of God. Missionaries, as well as others, will have to learn to "hang loose" as far as location is concerned—and even as far as the nature of their work or the length of their service is concerned. A sovereign God must have his freedom to move us wherever he wills, and neither we who are moved nor those who behold our moving have a right to evaluate our spirituality in terms of the particular location in which we serve or the duration of time we spend there.

All of this is to say that the current trend in missions toward short-term contracts does not represent spiritual deterioration, nor the abject surrender by mission boards to people's unwillingness (because of a "lack of faith") to commit themselves for a longer period of time. Instead, we have come to see the work of the Lord as a worldwide work, with the Lord's army a fluid and mobile instrument.

In some cases he may want to keep his soldiers in a given place over a period of many years, doing for a lifetime the same type of thing for which they first went to that particular place. In other instances, he may want to move his servants frequently, thrusting them into places of greater need or greater opportunity, shuttling them back and forth to their homeland when the demands of their families or other legitimate concerns make this advisable, giving them a sense of ministry wherever they are and the sweet contentment that comes from knowing that their fruitfulness is not determined by the length of their service in a particular place.

When Henry Martyn traveled from England to India by ship, the trip took many months and included a stop on the coast of South America. Now that trip would be made by air in a few hours. Martyn knew he could not return home soon, if **33** ever. But today transportation is different, and surely God wants us to serve him with a twentieth-century mentality.

Jungle Doctor

Second, *missions are thought to be limited to a very few kinds of activity.* Here the idea is that missionary work is carried on through only a few traditional approaches: teaching, preaching, medical work and related ministries. Such a limited concept is in our day almost a heresy, yet many earnest Christians still cling to it. How did we come to such an inadequate understanding of missions?

Some of us had exposure to missions from childhood days, so for years we have tended to think of missionary outreach in the same terms in which we first learned about it. Years ago, the missionaries we met or heard about seemed to be chiefly occupied as preachers of the gospel or as teachers of the "native" Christians or as doctors and nurses, ministering to physical and spiritual illnesses. To us, these things—and nothing else—constituted "missionary work."

And this is no small thing. A misunderstanding at this point leads to a very inadequate prayer life, which manifests itself in a routine kind of intercession on behalf of a stereotyped kind of missionary. By our limited concepts we are also robbed of the excitement of seeing what God is really doing in the world today. Our gifts tend to be designated for traditional forms of missionary enterprise only. And a great host of people, who might find their own place in what God is doing if they understood

34

how many places there are and what a variety of gifts and approaches he uses, are denied the spiritual satisfaction of being linked with Christ in this great task.

It is time to face frankly the mythical nature of our beliefs along these lines and begin to correct them in the light of the Scriptures and of present-day missionary experience.

To be sure, many people in the church today have a better comprehension of the great variety of missionary activities than did any previous generation. Twenty or thirty years ago, if a man did not feel that he could preach, teach or heal, he was not likely to feel "called" to missionary service. There was a strong feeling that other types of missionary activity were largely carried on by those in the "liberal" camp, and that they had got into these things because they had long since lost their primary impulse for evangelism and were now settling for secondary forms of service.

I can remember hearing as a teenager about an agricultural work being carried on in India by one of the old-line denominational missions. It was a tremendous project. But the Christians I knew and admired seemed to feel that this kind of thing went beyond the bounds of "real" missionary work, that such an approach was not very "spiritual," that in any case it could be justified only if it produced a "harvest of souls for Christ," and that the great danger was that this sort of missionary activity ministered so much to the body of man that the needs of his soul were inevitably overlooked.

So this project, in our thinking, was "liberal"   35

missionary work, and while we might be allowed to admire the dedication and self-abnegation of those who engaged in it, we knew we were not called to follow in their steps. Rather, we were encouraged to maintain our suspicions of such work and to seek a higher calling.

Multipronged Approach

Later, evangelical missions began to wake up to the fact that a multipronged approach is needed for the spread of the gospel, and that God's compassion for man extends to every area of human need—both "spiritual" needs and physical needs. We saw that we had sometimes made a sub-biblical distinction between these two categories. We also learned that God could use many different types of people in many more categories of ministry than we had previously considered to be truly "missionary."

We made room, after a while, for literature workers and came to see that a man who could neither preach nor heal might still be a very effective servant of the Lord in other lands as an ambassador of the printed page. We stretched our minds and our hearts enough to acknowledge that bookstore workers might be just as much "missionaries" as those to whom we had traditionally given that honored title.

Again, with the impact of radio and television in North America there came to us an increasing consciousness that God had put new tools in our hands in this generation and that we would be accountable to him if we did not make the fullest possible use of them. Needed, therefore, were not only technicians who could build and maintain radio stations and other professionals who could produce acceptable programs for them, but also communications specialists who would help us size up our audiences, evaluate our program resources and learn how best to get our message across to our hearers.

Would these communications specialists and other professionals and technicians who worked with them, motivated by the love of Christ for their fellow men, then be called missionaries? Of course, but we would have to stretch our concepts once again to make this possible!

Other wonderful tools were placed at our disposal, and the airplane was soon seen as an ally of the gospel as well as a means for taking Coca-Cola and Singer sewing machines to every part of the world. God gave us consecrated pilots and mechanics who put their gifts, their training and their experience at the service of the missionary enterprise, and once again the term "missionary" had to stretch.

This was only the beginning, and yet some people in the churches in the homeland never got this far. They still saw the missionary as the traditional pioneer, trekking through the jungle in a pith helmet, preaching to groups and individuals, administering physical and spiritual first aid.

Professional Specialists
God has opened up other approaches, too, in recent years—places where personnel and funds are desperately needed and where work that is just as 37

truly missionary work as the traditional variety is being effectively carried on.

What shall we say, for example, of the need for workers among students in all parts of the Third World? With the increase in student population, with the questing of high school and college students for the reality that is found only in Jesus Christ, something more than the average run of preachers, teachers or medical workers is needed. God is beginning to raise up men and women who have special gifts for this task, who have gained a real measure of experience in it in the homeland, and who are as truly missionaries as any of the servants of God in former generations.

Those of us who have served the Lord in other lands know how in recent years consecrated agronomists have found a ministry for Christ in many places where the gospel is scarcely known. We have watched them in action, seen their reception by needy people, noted the effective way in which they have ministered both to physical and to spiritual needs and rejoiced that God has in our day called such people to the service of missions. To be sure, they do not fit the old categories of missionary service too well, but this is more a reflection on our categories than on our workers.

You would be impressed, as I have been, by the tremendous ministry of a man who is at the same time a missionary in the fullest sense of the word and a competent consulting psychologist, as he uses his gifts and experience for the glory of Christ and for the meeting of human needs in Latin America. This is a relatively new field of missionary service, but one that has been so richly blessed of the Lord that no one can deny its real and potential effectiveness in the service of Christ.

I think of social workers who have brought to our own mission an expertise that some of our older missionaries did not have in dealing with the problems of broken families, of retarded children, of homeless youngsters. These have carried on their ministry in the name of Christ, motivated by his love and characterized by his compassion. They are missionaries of a special breed, and they remind us again of the multiple facets of the missionary approach in our time.

But these are only a few of the many ways in which God is using his servants today, and we need to keep stretching our thinking in order to take in the new approaches which the Lord is using in carrying out his purposes. God is giving us trained business administrators, who are as truly missionaries as any of the rest of us; youth specialists, who bring something to camp and club work which goes far beyond the limited knowledge and experience of the traditional missionary; literacy experts, whose work leads people into the riches of the Word of God and into a whole new world of education which fits them to provide more adequately for their families than ever before. All this in the name of Christ and of missions!

Some years ago, in speaking to an Inter-Varsity group, I dared to say that God could use any kind of professional training as a form of missionary activity, if the individual having such background was yielded to him. After the meeting a student chal-   **39** lenged my statement, saying that he was a major in grain marketing and he did not see how *that* could be used on the mission field. He caught me off my guard, and I had to confess that I, too, was puzzled by his situation. I acknowledged that my statement was too sweeping.

Sometime later, when we were desperately in need of administrative help in our mission, I was approached by a consecrated layman who offered to leave his secular employment and become a missionary, if he could be of help to us. When I asked him what his business background was, he said, "Grain marketing"!

He did come with us, and the administrative skills and experience developed in grain marketing proved to be completely transferable to the work of the Lord. He serves the mission today in a most effective way. Is he a missionary? Not if we believe the old myth of the limited call. But if we have learned that God can use all kinds of gifts, all kinds of experiences, in all kinds of work for the spread of the gospel, then he most assuredly is a missionary. He knows that he is sent of God to help make Christ known; he meets the biblical standard for a missionary.

The church of Jesus Christ in the homeland must learn to revise its concept of missionary work and to enlarge its understanding of what is involved in making Christ known in a day like this. The people of God must be led to see that our Lord has infinite resources for the accomplishment of his purposes, and that he has placed those resources in the church of Jesus Christ. Christians need to know that missionary work is a work of infinite variety in which every believer may find his place.

All this is to say that the idea that the missionary call is for a very limited number of people, with very special gifts, which qualify them for a very limited kind of activity, and even then only if they have not passed the age of thirty—all of this is a myth, detrimental to the work of the Lord and an unnecessary limitation on our comprehension of the purposes of God in our time. Like the other myths about missions, it must not only be denied; it must be destroyed.

4

THE MYTH
OF THE FINISHED
TASK

You won't hear it from the pulpit very often, and no missionary conference ever uses it as a theme, but many a church member believes it today: "The day of missions is past!"

This idea has been communicated to us in a variety of ways; we have heard it stated so often and so convincingly that many are strongly disposed to believe it.

Sometimes it appears in the guise of a kind of triumphalism—the idea that the job of missions has been so widely carried out and so well prosecuted that we can now retire from the field with the satisfaction that the major task of making Christ known to all men is now accomplished; we can pack our bags and go home, congratulating ourselves on a job well done.

In this form, it represents a sort of religious counterpart to the attitude recommended some years ago by Senator George Aiken of Vermont, who said that the way to get out of Vietnam was to "say that we have won, and go home!" Such advice seems to be applied by some Christians to the missionary situation today: "Let's pat ourselves on the back for the job we've done—and walk away from it. The day of missions is past!"

Others try to convince us that missions in today's world are an anachronism, since religious pluralism is a fact of life everywhere and we've come to the place where we recognize that every man's religion or lack of it is his own business, not to be interfered with by zealots of another faith.

The myth is stated in a variety of ways. But the meaning is the same: It's time to retrench, to withdraw, to retire completely from the field of missionary activity. The amazing thing is that this counsel comes largely from within the church itself. It is not the cry of ungodly men, vehemently screaming, "Missionaries, go home!" Instead it comes from the lips of professing Christians.

The idea that the missionary task is finished frequently takes the form of a statement that missionaries are no longer wanted or needed, and it is this particular concept that we want to take a close look at here. There are many voices telling us that missionaries are no longer *wanted* today throughout the world. This attitude is often attributed to the rising spirit of nationalism which characterizes so many of the lands we knew as "mission fields."

That such a spirit of nationalism exists, and that

it is often marked by a growing sense of independence and self-sufficiency, no one can deny. Canon Burgess Carr, general secretary of the All-African Conference of Churches, manifests such a spirit when he says, "The sooner the traditional expatriate is out, the better.... African churches must come to grips with standing on our own feet. We need a moratorium on missionaries if we are going to develop a really true African church."[1]

Moreover, it must be readily granted that such a spirit of nationalism can be a very constructive thing, and that the idea that these nations no longer welcome outside help—especially in the realm of religion—sounds very rational. Besides, the realization that such an awakening consciousness of national identity may reflect credit, rather than blame, on the missionary cause makes it easier for some Christians to accept.

Again, it is said that missionaries are no longer wanted in many lands because their well-meaning but insensitive approaches in days gone by have barred the doors to their return. In some of these lands, missionaries have seemed more like the agents of an unwanted colonialism than like heralds of hope, and on occasion they have even been thought of as a religious counterpart to the much hated C.I.A.

The attitudes of some missionaries, our accusers say, have been marked by an overweening paternalism toward young Christians and national churches, and there is strong agreement that there is no place now, if there ever was one, for such attitudes.

45

If these charges are exaggerated, they are certainly not without substance. On the basis of these accusations we are often told that missionaries are not wanted in most parts of the world today. This is just another way of saying that, for those areas at least, the day of missions is past.

Beyond this, it is frequently insisted that missionaries are no longer *needed* today. Glowing stories are told about how the church has now been planted in every part of the world. We are reminded that these new churches need to be left alone to work out their own destinies, to root themselves in their own soil, to become what God wants them to be, without the modifying and often harmful influences brought by missionaries who come from another culture and who tend to stifle the initiative of the young church by insisting they learn Western ways.

This reasoning, too, seems to make sense; the pioneer phase of missions is undoubtedly over in most of the world. Much of the work which the missionaries originally went to do has been accomplished. Their further intrusion on the scene, it seems to many, not only is not needed but is probably detrimental to the future of the church in these countries.

What shall we say to such claims? Whatever we say, let us not become defensive. We are not called by God to defend institutions and programs, however useful they may have been to people in another day. We are called as Christians to be continually seeking the most effective ways of making

the gospel of Christ known to the whole world in

our own day. If this means radical changes in our approach, so let it be. We are not called to struggle for the institutional survival of missionary agencies.

But too often we act as though we have been given just that kind of call. We become defensive about our methods and approaches, and we act as though the missionary enterprise as we have known it is the last, best hope for the church and the world.

On such occasions we become like the young lady who had recently graduated from a First Aid course. While returning home one night, she came upon the scene of a tragic accident. A car had swerved off the road and smashed into a tree; the driver lay on the ground in a pool of blood, apparently with no one paying any attention to his suffering. In recounting the experience later, she said, "When I saw him, I was surely thankful for my First Aid course and for such a wonderful opportunity to use it! I remembered that they had taught us that, whenever we felt ourselves in danger of fainting, we should put our heads down between our knees. I felt sick when I saw the battered driver, so I lowered my head—and I didn't faint! It's certainly a good thing that I had that First Aid course."

No, there is no need to plead for mere survival of the missionary enterprise as we have known it. If there is no longer a place for missionaries in some lands, we ought to be honest enough to admit it— and then to seek better ways to occupy ourselves in the service of Christ.

Do They Want Us?

We ought to admit that there are some places where missionaries are not wanted today. There are some closed doors. While the number of such places is not so large as it is usually believed to be, there are such areas in the world. In addition, some doors are closing. In countries like India, for example, we may be facing at least the temporary end of foreign missionary activity in the foreseeable future. And there are other places where missionaries are not welcome today for this very reason: National church leaders in these countries feel perfectly capable of running their own show and sincerely believe they can do it better unhampered by the presence of foreign missionaries.

It cannot be denied that in many parts of the world there has been a violent reaction against all forms of colonialism and paternalism, with the result that any foreign missionary is suspect. Many a missionary feels less appreciated in the country of his adoption today than he did a few years ago.

Beyond these reactions, we ought not to be surprised if there is also satanic opposition to the entrance of the light of Christ into areas that have long been in darkness. Whatever else we know about the devil and his strategies, we know that he always opposes the spread of Christ's liberating gospel and that he has a great variety of ways by which to implement his opposition.

We ought not to expect him to remain passive before the continued influx of witnessing Christians into lands that have long been his uncontested domain.

Let us be honest enough to admit, too, that there may be places where missionaries are not needed today. I write with less assurance here, because I am convinced that such places are very few and because the absence of need, even if real, may be a temporary condition—too temporary to be allowed to determine the missionary policy of the church.

Yet there may be some places where the indigenous church needs for a time to be utterly on its own, and there may be situations in the world where the presence of missionaries will handicap the work rather than help it. Even in lands where missionaries are still welcome, it often proves advisable to lower the profile of the Western sending organizations for the overall good of the work.

But, having admitted the partial validity of some of the arguments against missionary work today, we must now insist that they represent only a part of the truth—indeed only a small part of it, and so small a part that sweeping generalizations such as "The day of missions is over!" or "Missionaries are no longer wanted or needed!" are more myth than reality, even though they may contain elements of truth.

In many parts of the world missionaries are not only wanted but desperately wanted. This is not merely the opinion of mission executives, who are sometimes suspected of being concerned chiefly about the perpetuation of their own organizations, but of the leaders of the national churches and of our brothers in Christ who are his body in these lands. Certainly in Latin America we are continually faced by a demand for more missionaries. This demand is not fomented by candidate secretaries, eager to recruit, nor by heads of Christian schools in the homeland, who may feel that the success of their institutions is measured by the number of missionary candidates they send out.

Instead, it comes from those who head the national churches, who have carefully surveyed the spiritual needs of their own lands and realistically assessed the contribution that foreign missionaries can yet make to the work. It is these national leaders, fully aware of the limitations of missionary work but deeply conscious of the demands of the unfinished task among their own people, who have bombarded us with requests for additional missionary personnel—more requests than we have been able to fill.

At the Latin American Congress on Evangelism, held in Bogotá, Colombia, in 1969, some of us from the Latin America Mission had private sessions with the three largest delegations present: those from Brazil, Argentina and Chile. Our purpose was to learn from them the spiritual needs in their lands and to make ourselves available to the church of Christ in those countries, if they felt that there was any way in which our gifts, and particularly our experience in evangelism, could be of help to them. The response was overwhelming—it was characterized by a deep consciousness of spiritual need and an urgent plea for missionary reinforcements.

These who were speaking were the choice leaders of the church of Christ in their countries, and they made it plain that they would welcome all the missionary help we could give them.

The Community of Latin American Evangelical Ministries (the organization in Latin America with which our mission is affiliated), while largely under Latin leadership, is constantly seeking from us additional personnel from North America. The personnel lists which the Community has compiled tell, both by their length and by their variety, of continuing need for qualified missionaries from both north and south of the Rio Grande. These requests are urgent and insistent, and they are doubly significant because they come from the Latins themselves.

Nor is our experience unique in this regard; many another mission bears a similar witness: more personnel needs than they can fill, with the pressure for help originating not with the missionaries but with the national churches. It is no exaggeration to say that, for every area where missionaries are no longer wanted, there are dozens of places where their presence is both requested and urged.

A New Role

Missionary organizations are finding that the increasing emergence of strong leadership in the national churches does not diminish the call for foreign missionaries; it only seems to accentuate that demand, while at the same time modifying considerably the role of the missionary. The need for the services of the missionary who can adapt 51 himself to such a role has increased, rather than lessened.

In the light of that last statement, my declaration that missionaries are still desperately wanted in many places should be qualified in at least two respects. First of all, they are wanted only *if they can meet the standards of the national church*. The time is long past when we can do all our candidate screening in the sending countries and then dump on the national churches the fruit of our recruiting efforts, with a gesture that seems to say, "Here they are, you lucky people!"

We must learn to give the national church full and usually final say in the acceptance or rejection of the foreigners who seek to work with them. They want missionary help, but they want the kind that they can approve, after careful investigation of their own. A maturing church has every right to this prerogative, which we have too long denied it.

Second, these missionaries are wanted only *if they can give clear evidence that they have learned from the mistakes of the past and that they are ready to turn over both authority and responsibility for the work to their national brethren.* This matter will be touched on more fully in a later chapter, but let it be said here and now that the *only* kind of missionary who continues to be needed is the one who not only knows how to work *with* and *under* his national brethren but also is eager to do so.

This is not easy; there is no great supply of such people, but God is in the business of delivering us from our self-centeredness and our cultural cockiness, and he delights to make us servants in the likeness of Christ, if we will only allow him to do so.

Not only are missionaries wanted in many parts of the world; they are needed. They are needed, first of all, to fulfill the New Testament ideal of the church of Christ—a body of believers in which the middle walls of partition have been broken down, and where Jews, Gentiles, Barbarians, Scythians, bond and free are brought together by the blood of Christ in a unity which is rare on earth because no merely human organization can either produce or maintain it.

The Church Is International

The Latin American church needs to be thoroughly and completely rooted in Latin America and to be guided and directed by Latin Americans, not by those who come from another culture. But at its best, the Latin American church will not be composed solely of Latin Americans. In like fashion, the North American and European church needs to be rooted in its own culture, not an exotic one—but it will be most effective for Christ when it also has the input of Latin Americans, Asians and Africans who have been redeemed by the same gospel and who now make their God-given gifts available to other churches in North America and Europe as well as in their homelands.

It cannot be said too often: The New Testament ideal is not ethnic or cultural exclusiveness in the church of Christ, but a partnership that demonstrates the power of the Good News and that makes 53 its outreach infinitely more effective.

Moreover, according to those who direct the church of Christ in these lands, missionaries are still needed in considerable numbers to provide skills and experience not yet fully available to the local churches otherwise. To say this is not to imply in any sense a superiority of foreign missionaries over national Christians. In character, culture and Christian experience, national Christians often surpass the best of missionaries. We have much to learn from them, and there are some things they can do infinitely better than we can. But the fact remains—and no one acknowledges it more quickly than the nationals themselves—that their churches and their evangelistic outreach are strengthened when they have the help of the skills and training of qualified foreign missionaries whom God sends their way. The developing church abroad can still profit from the long centuries of Christian tradition and the extensive training and experience which, by the grace of God, have been the heritage of many believers in the West.

Finally, missionaries are needed to help get a gigantic task done. By any reckoning, the commission to give every man everywhere an opportunity to know Christ is a task of awesome proportions, even in an age when a multitude of new inventions is available to expedite the enterprise.

My hosts took me one evening at midnight to see Mexico City from the tower of the city's tallest skyscraper. As I looked out on the twinkling lights **54** which represented the dwellings of some seven million people, I was filled with wonder at the beauty of the spectacle—until I began to think of what it would take to evangelize effectively that one city.

I remembered how I had thrilled at the expressed desire of Christians in Mexico City to get the gospel into every home, and how glad I was that they had asked us to help them. But suddenly the enormity of it all came over me, and I fell into a state of burden that bordered on depression. I realized, as I never had before, that the fulfillment of the Great Commission in any area of the world demands an outpouring of the power of God and the readiness of the church to use every available resource for the accomplishment of the task.

Throughout the world, national leadership in the churches has long since come to the same realization. National leaders do not seek to escape responsibility for the evangelization of their lands, but they know they will need all the help they can get—from God and from man—if they are ever to confront their generation with the Good News of Christ.

No one claims that such a gigantic undertaking is ever to be accomplished merely by the multiplication of foreign missionaries, although on occasion overenthusiastic missionary leaders have sounded as though they thought this was the key to ultimate success. Nor does anyone really believe that merely multiplying the number of national pastors in these areas will accomplish the desired result—much as such an increase is needed.

Most national church leaders and mission leaders are coming to see what Evangelism-in-Depth, New Life for All and similar movements have been telling us for some time: The only hope of total evangelization lies in total mobilization—all the church must be trained and thrust into this enormous task. But this literally means *all* the church, with the church in the West putting its resources of funds and personnel at the disposal of the churches in other lands, and with those churches sharing their God-given resources with us as well.

The fact of the matter is that every land needs missionaries. People in North America who are shocked when they hear that Latin America is beginning to send missionaries to us are shocked only because they are unaware of the resources God has given his church in other parts of the world, and equally unaware of our own desperate need here. By the same token, as long as we have something that Latin America wants and needs, we must provide it—*on their terms and for their use.*

Missions in our day is a two-way street, and every land where Christ is known is meant to be both a sending and a receiving country. Every church, however weak and needy, is called both to teach God's truth to others and to learn God's truth from others. And every Christian is meant by God to be both a recipient and a transmitter of the Good News.

When churches all over the world need and want help, it is a disservice to Christ to perpetuate the myth that "the day of missions is over." It is likewise dangerous and misleading to disseminate the idea that missionaries are no longer wanted or needed. These ideas are heresies, part of the myths that have grown up around missions in our time, and they ought to be exposed as such wherever men name the name of Christ. To do less is to fail our Lord and to help undermine the cause which is nearest to his heart.

5

THE MYTH
OF THE
UNFINISHABLE TASK

The church secretary, typing out the copy for Sunday's bulletin, struck only one wrong key, but as a result the hymn "Rise Up, O Men of God" was announced as "Wise Up, O Men of God"—and perhaps was even more relevant because of her mistake.

Another curious error crept into a bibliography a few years ago when a new book on missions, *Facing the Unfinished Task*, was listed as *Facing the Unfinishable Task*!

By his mistake that typesetter actually gave expression to the feelings of a good many Christians. It wouldn't be polite to admit it, but a surprising number of God's people have come to the conclusion, down deep in their hearts, that Christ gave us an impossible job. This business of taking the gospel to every creature is a never-ending task, they have decided. Its proportions are overwhelming, even paralyzing, and so these Christians wind up by believing that Christ was just dangling a high ideal before his disciples—one which he must have known could never really be carried out.

Voices of Despair

Interestingly enough, some Roman Catholic leaders are extremely vocal in their expression of this sort of despair. Father Prudencio Damboriena, S.J., puts it this way: "Today discouragement [in Catholic mission circles] has gained frightening momentum. Mission stations are being abandoned, and replacements do not arrive to fill the vacancies."[1] Father Damboriena goes on to say that many Catholic missiologists agree with K.M. Pannikar that "the attempt to convert Asia has definitely failed," and then comments that "in the main... the role of the missionary around the world is on the decline."[2] It would appear that among Catholics as well as Protestants there are loud voices which proclaim that the day of missions is past.

Dr. Arthur Glasser, writing about the position taken by Donald Dawe of Union Theological Seminary, Richmond, Virginia, comments: "With no attempt at documentation, Dawe affirms that the outcome of missions, as with America's foreign aid program, has been 'frustration and failure.' As for the church in Asia, Africa, and Latin America, he dolefully concludes that 'future prospects are not promising.' "[3]

Even among evangelicals there seems to be an amazing amount of pessimism concerning the future of the missionary enterprise, particularly with regard to the home church's willingness to support it. Dr. Harold Lindsell, editor of *Christianity Today*, has written: "In the present situation, any hope for a breakthrough or a dynamic advance by the evangelical churches is minimal. Given present trends, all we can anticipate is a continuation of the current evangelical pace, if not a substantial slow-down."[4]

If this idea of the unfinishable task is another myth that needs to be exposed, we had better first admit that there are plenty of seemingly logical reasons for giving it credence. One has only to look at the statistics on population growth to be overawed by the dimensions of our missionary task. Those who attended the World Congress on Evangelism (Berlin, 1966) may long since have forgotten most of the speeches and papers, but none of them can forget the great "population clock" which dominated the lobby of the congress hall. Its remorseless ticking, conveying by the rapidly changing figures on its face not only the passing of time but also the inordinate growth of the human family, left an indelible impression on all who saw it. How could our best-intentioned efforts to preach the gospel to every creature ever catch up with such a runaway population growth?

Besides, if you have ever attended missionary conferences, you are well aware that the appeal is ever the same, year after year: always a cry for more personnel, more funds, to do a job which forever   61 seems larger than it was when the previous report was given. No wonder we find it easy to believe the myth of the unfinishable task! No wonder that after a while a sense of "What's the use?" grips us, and we begin to look around for tasks that are of more manageable proportions! Why knock yourself out on a job that can never be finished anyway?

It doesn't look like a myth, this idea of the unfinishable task, but surely we have learned long since that myths do not usually advertise themselves as such. And before we accept it as truth and become victims of the spiritual paralysis which so often results, we had better take another look at the evidence.

Christ's Expectation

Note, in the first place, that Christ never gave the slightest hint that he thought the job could not be done. In the Great Commission, he recognizes that his disciples *will* be going into all the world and he *commands* them to make disciples of every nation.[5] There is a note of high seriousness about his words; any idea that he is merely challenging his disciples by dangling before them an unattainable ideal has to be read into the passage. There is nothing in Christ's words to give credibility to such an idea.

Again, when he charged his disciples with the task of witnessing to the ends of the earth (Acts 1:8), there is every reason to believe that he thought it could be done. On some occasions in his teaching, Christ spoke in the hyperbole so dear to the Eastern

mind (the camel going through the eye of the

needle; the log in a man's eye). But there is no exaggeration here; Jerusalem is to be evangelized, and so are Judea and Samaria and the uttermost parts of the earth.

Moreover, when our Lord spoke of his return in Matthew 24:14, he clearly linked it with a prior preaching of the gospel to all the nations. He obviously had full confidence that at some future date he would come again. He was equally confident that before that great moment in history the Good News would be carried to every part of the earth.

It all comes down to this: Either Christ was deceived in believing that the job can be done, or we have been deceived in believing that it cannot. Knowing full well our own capacity for being deceived, it ought to be very easy for us to accept the fact that we have believed a myth, while Christ has been utterly trustworthy, as always.

While we need no greater authority than Christ's own word, there is abundant additional evidence that we have been wrong in thinking that the task is unfinishable.

Look at church history, for example. Any objective view of it leaves the unmistakable impression that the most glorious moments the church has known have been those when she took seriously the commission of her Lord and once again set about the evangelization of the world. Watch as the church again and again has become self-centered and preoccupied with her own needs, indifferent to the spiritual destitution of the rest of the world. Then behold how, again and again, the Spirit of God has wooed his people back to his Word and to his will—which all the while had been the evangelization of the world. See the comatose church suddenly become alive again; watch self-centered Christians suddenly throw off the shackles of their own selfishness; behold men and women spending themselves unstintingly for the spread of the gospel of Christ.

The history of missions is the story of men and women who have taken Christ seriously; who have recognized that they have been richly blessed in order that others, through them, might be blessed; who have known that God can use a handful of dedicated servants to storm successfully the territory which Satan has usurped. So they have gone out, terrible as an army with banners, sometimes experiencing glorious victory, sometimes knowing inglorious defeat, but always sustained and fortified by the assurance that the evangelization of the world is God's will and that his church is really pleasing to him only when it is busy about that task.

Another element which brings great encouragement as we face the challenge of world evangelization is the fact that wonderful new instruments of mass communication have been provided for us within recent years. The worldwide dissemination of truth (and of error, as well) has been tremendously facilitated in our time, and any careful observer of these developments knows that there is much greater possibility of reaching every creature on the earth with a particular message now than was the case in any preceding generation.

Obviously, it is not necessary to be a Christian in order to appreciate the impact on society of accelerated transportation, multiplied channels of communication and linguistic advances. But to the Christian, concerned that the message of life in Christ shall be given to every man everywhere, these scientific developments of recent years have a special significance.

He readily acknowledges that these discoveries are neutral in themselves: Their potential for evil is as great as that for good. And he sees in them not gimmicks which guarantee the successful completion of the missionary task, but rather implements put at his disposal by a sovereign God for the accomplishment of the purpose for which the church of Christ exists—the making known of his saving gospel to every man and every nation.

Travel

Who can measure, for example, what the invention of the airplane has meant to the rapid and effective spread of God's truth? True, in the hands of warmakers, it can be used to rain death and destruction on great areas of the earth. But put at the disposal of God's servants, the plane becomes a means of penetration of the unreached regions of the world with the good news that Christ has died and risen again and that men can be reconciled to God and to their fellow men through him.

And so, as I write these lines, primitive peoples in distant places around the world, utterly untouched by the gospel through all these centuries, are hacking out airstrips in the jungle, and by the time you read these words missionary airplanes will be landing on those airstrips, bringing medi-   65 cine for the sick, contact with the outside world from which these people have always been isolated, and best of all a Savior and a Book. For the first time these tribes and villages will come to know Christians who will demonstrate the love of Christ and proclaim his gospel to people who could never have any eternal hope apart from that saving message.

How Paul would have welcomed the speed of our modern means of transportation! He would have seen in such a factor the possibility of visiting his beloved churches more frequently and for longer periods of time. He would have rejoiced in the hope of pressing on, on, on—to where Christ had never been named—because he was now unshackled from the terrible limitations of earthbound travel as he had known it.

Communications

Stand with me on the curb of a center-city street in LaPaz, Bolivia. A parade is passing by—thousands of Bolivians publicly testifying to their faith in Jesus Christ, as they mark the close of a year-long effort to bring the gospel of Christ to every home in their needy land. Note with me that most of the people in the parade are Indians, many of them very, very poor, many of them terribly undernourished.

But note, too, that the great majority of them are carrying transistor radios! These imports from Japan are relatively cheap in Bolivia, but their purchase price has meant great sacrifice for these

66 Indians. As they march, they are listening to Christian hymns and martial music, broadcast to help them proceed in orderly array through the heart of the capital city.

Tomorrow the parade will be over and the Indians will have returned to their scattered villages, but these same little miracle instruments of modern technology will be bringing them, and many others besides, the message of God. The Good News of Christ's death and resurrection will be readily available to them and to their fellow countrymen in a sense that was never true in earlier generations.

All over the Andean mountainsides, into the humblest and most isolated of dwellings, into the high-rise apartments, the luxury hotels and the slum hovels of the capital city, the message of life in Christ penetrates where it has never gone before. Suddenly one knows that, in a modern revolution he has long since taken for granted, there is a miracle, a miracle given by God to aid in the worldwide dissemination of his truth to all men. Seeing this, one can only thank God and take courage, knowing that the church's task *can* be finished.

Think, too, of all the other recent developments in the realm of communications. We dare not lose our sense of wonder over satellites and television, cassettes and transistors—a sense of wonder arising not merely out of the realization of what science has accomplished, but out of a conviction that a sovereign God, more burdened than we could ever be for the evangelization of the world, has had a hand in all this.

A Mobilized Church

But there is another encouraging factor which ought to be mentioned here, a worldwide phenomenon that has manifested itself only recently. I refer to the way in which the church of Christ in many parts of the world has recently begun to mobilize itself for the accomplishment of the task.

In the fall of 1969, a group of about thirty men were called together from all over the world to discuss what God was doing through the evangelistic efforts of the church in the lands from which they came. The consultation was held in Switzerland and it lasted for about a week. Participating were nationals from a dozen countries. Our purpose was to learn from each other, both by the recounting of successes and by the confessing of failures. The consultation was also intended to help us understand, through our ministry to one another, how we can more effectively do his will in evangelism. It was an amazing experience. For one thing, after all the reports had been given, we noted that, while we had not been asked to confine our presentations to any particular period in history, the reports showed that the wonderful new developments in evangelism which were so exciting to all of us had come to pass in about ten years' time, chiefly during the decade of the sixties.

We heard about Evangelism-in-Depth in Latin America, New Life for All in Nigeria, Christ for All in the Congo, Evangelism Deep and Wide in Vietnam, and similar encouraging reports from Korea, Japan, India, the United States and elsewhere. Obviously, there was much variety in the methodology of these movements. And they had no single origin. But it became evident to us that all of these programs, which God had raised up in recent days, had much in common.

For one thing, it became apparent that the Lord's people in many parts of the world had come to a fresh conviction that their areas could be completely and thoroughly evangelized—in the sense that a meaningful, persuasive presentation of the gospel could be given to every creature in our day. This conviction was not a mere momentary emotional response to the Great Commission, such as churches and Christians have had on many previous occasions, but a deep commitment to the doing of a seemingly impossible task in the confidence that God has willed the evangelization of the world and that he will enable us to accomplish it.

But there was more than this. In each place there had been a frank recognition of the enormous dimensions of the task. This was something to be done not just by a spiritual elite called "missionaries," or a similarly gifted group called "national pastors." The task of total evangelism would not be accomplished merely by multiplying the numbers of these two groups.

Instead, *every member* of the church of Christ would have to be mobilized and then trained, so that he could and would share the gospel with those whom God wanted to reach. And so they had set themselves to this task of teaching the biblical truth concerning the individual believer's part in world evangelization. And they had not only exhorted the believers to do the job; they had trained **69** them for it. Result: All over the world (with varying degrees of success, to be sure, but to an extent never before realized) the people of God had come to a new understanding of their privilege and responsibility as witnesses and had moved out in carefully prepared programs with the object of reaching every home and every heart with the gospel of Christ.

Nobody claimed complete success. No one insisted that in his area every person had now been confronted with the claims of Christ. There was no air of shallow triumphalism about the reports. But without exception certain elements were stressed: The church in each area was awake to its God-given call to evangelize its part of the world; a great measure of blessing and fruitfulness had been experienced as lay believers in large numbers had been mobilized, trained and thrust forth in evangelistic witness; there was, on the basis of renewed confidence in God's Word and the results already achieved in tackling the awesome task, a deep conviction that the goal of total evangelization was attainable—in our day!

We came away from the consultation in Switzerland not with a momentary upsurge of evangelistic enthusiasm, but with the joy of knowing that God had permitted us to be a part of a great and special thing he is doing in our time. Moreover, the fact that this conviction was shared by our brethren from many parts of the world, as a result of their current experiences, gave it special validity and provided us with great incentive to expect even

more wonderful things in the years ahead.

And so we cannot accept the myth of the unfinishable task. God's Word assures us that it is his purpose to gather his church from every nation of the earth. He has put in our hands the tools for the task, including modern means of transportation and a great variety of effective media. He has quickened his church in our time, blessing it with a fresh devotion to himself and a fresh commitment to giving every person the opportunity of knowing Christ. The task is finishable, and God calls us to give ourselves to it—now!

THE MYTH
OF THE LIMITED GOAL

Throughout this century, the missionary enterprise has been dominated by the thought that its ultimate achievement would be in terms of the establishment of indigenous churches. The term *indigenous church* came by tradition to be defined as a church which was self-governing, self-propagating and self-supporting. This ideal has been stated so often that it has been accepted by great numbers of Christians. It has even gathered around itself an air of sanctity; it has become a holy tradition, a seemingly biblical ideal. And like the other myths we have dealt with, it has enough truth in it to make it attractive—and persistent!

Undoubtedly the emphasis upon such a concept was a reaction against the unwise paternalism which had often been characteristic of the missionary enterprise. Mission strategists awakened painfully to the fact that, in the name of Christ, we had often been building our own cultural empires and subjecting new Christians to a form of colonialism that was never justified and could no longer be defended.

Churches had been established, but they were kept in a state of unending dependency on the foreign mission, and they were considered successful if they looked like replicas of the churches where the mission had its home headquarters, using Western music and forms of worship. None too soon, we awakened to the shallowness and self-defeating nature of such a concept.

Then, as a result of our usual human tendency to overreact, the pendulum swung violently in the other direction, and the new emphasis was on missionaries planting indigenous churches, working themselves out of jobs, removing the scaffolding of their activity as soon as the building was "finished." Soon, a body of literature had sprung up around these concepts, and they were repeated so frequently by missionary leaders, pastors and others that they became accepted as though they had the validity and authority of biblical truth.

Let it be readily admitted that a reaction against paternalism and colonialism was long since overdue, and if an emphasis on the indigenous church as the ultimate ideal helped to dispel these earlier myths, then it was helpful, even if terribly limited. There is considerable evidence, however, that what we really did was to substitute a new myth for the old one. We set a goal that lay far short of the one God has established for his church. Our ambition was too limited; we were ready to settle for much less than God wanted of us.

Self-Sufficient

The problem undoubtedly lay in the inadequate and unbiblical definition of the word indigenous. As we have seen, it had come to mean, in a popular sense, a church that fulfilled the "three-self" formula: self-government, self-support, self-propagation. This formula became so current among us that it was soon accepted uncritically, and there were probably even those who thought it could be found in the Bible, if one looked hard enough!

There were several things wrong with that formula. Certainly, it put an unbiblical stress on "self," as Beyerhaus and Lefever point out when they say, "The New Testament speaks of 'self' only as something to be denied, or at least as something only to be discovered through being set aside and forgotten."[1] Beyerhaus had also shown the inadequacy of this ideal in an article in the International Review of Missions almost ten years ago. Others have reminded us more recently that the Bible not only underplays but even condemns an emphasis on the self, in the sense in which we are using that term here.

It is relatively easy to demonstrate from Scripture that the gospel is meant to be the death knell of our self-effort (Eph. 2:8-9); the biblical picture of our bankruptcy leaves no room for self-confidence in spiritual affairs (Rom. 3:23); the death and resurrection of Christ are intended to deliver us from self-centeredness (2 Cor. 5:14-15).

Independent

In addition, this limited concept of the indigenous principle takes the legitimate ideal of independency and pushes it to unbiblical extremes; it really reflects the unscriptural individualism of our Western culture more than it does any truly biblical pattern. To be sure, the church of Jesus Christ is meant to be independent of an unwise paternalism, but there is a sort of independency which is not of God and which represents a great danger for the church.

Obviously, we are never meant to be independent of the Lord himself, but another and perhaps even more subtle danger exists for us, in the cultivation of a sense of independency which cuts us off from other members of the body of Jesus Christ. The apostle Paul's clear teaching with regard to the interdependency of the various members of the body—the fact that we are *supposed* to need and complement each other—is overlooked by many Christians.

A further result of this myth is that it tends to make the local church an end in itself. It gives the impression that when this newly established body of believers has attained a certain status in government, in support and in growth, it has done its duty. It makes survival of the local unit on an independent basis the ultimate criterion of success, and implicitly creates the impression that when it can function on its own it has accomplished the purpose of its existence. No wonder, in the light of this sort of teaching, that so many churches founded by missionaries seem to have no missionary spirit of their own! We have taught believers to be self-satisfied the moment they are legitimately able to claim independence.

Since we have taught them that this is the highest ideal, why should we be so surprised when they see no reason to go beyond it? As Beyerhaus and Lefever put it, "A church which feels that its own responsibility has been discharged when the new church is established as a self-governing, and wholly or largely self-supporting body, has never rightly understood its missionary responsibility. 'If you want to go home when we have achieved a responsible existence of our own, you should never have come,' said the Asian Christian leader, Dr. D. T. Niles, not long ago."[2]

Sound but Sterile

With such a limited goal, it is inevitable that we produce churches that are deficient in missionary passion like so many orthodox, fundamental, "indigenous" churches in the West, which are sound but sterile. Even where missionary concern is not completely absent, churches that have been taught this "indigenous ideal" seem to consider their participation in the missionary enterprise as an extra feature added to their church life—a supplement, a luxury, an option, instead of the primary reason for their existence.

It is fortunate that missionary thinkers are beginning to protest the inadequacy of the "three-self" emphasis as an ideal for a Christian church. Peter Wagner, for example, sets the goal not as the indigenous church but as the "mature church," which 77 he describes in these words: "A mature church is successfully discipling the non-Christians in its own community.... Not only does it grow as a congregation, but the mature church sends forth people to plant daughter churches in neighboring communities. Finally, it has developed a cross-cultural vision for planting churches in other cultures, whether near or far. This final step is one of the most advanced signs of maturity"—which he admits is "not yet common enough in the Third World."[3]

It is to be hoped that the writings of these men will set us on a new course and help us overcome some of the deadly consequences of the unbiblical teaching which has passed uncriticized in our circles for so long.

Indeed, the biblical position is very different from that which we have taught and practiced. It is not necessary for us to deny the importance of self-government, self-support and self-propagation in order to see that there is a much higher ideal than this which God holds for his church. The Scriptures clearly teach that God saves us as individuals in order that other individuals might be saved. He puts in our hands the bread of life, as he put it in the hands of the disciples long ago, not only so that we may have adequate nutrition but also so that the multitudes may be fed.

It is not enough, in the biblical view, for us to receive the blessings of God and be thankful. We have not fulfilled our destiny until we have become directly involved in this task of making Christ known and of feeding the multitudes. Not all of us are called to be evangelists, in the limited and technical sense of that term, but we are all called to be witnesses, and we do not fulfil our calling merely by banding together with other like-minded believers to enjoy the benefits of independency or even the sweetness of Christian fellowship.

Likewise, God plants churches in order that they may plant other churches. Again and again, reproduction is seen as the goal in the Scriptures. It is just as important in the spiritual realm that we be fruitful and multiply as it is in the physical realm. We are not called to mere survival; we are called to establish other bodies of believers, and any lesser goal falls short of the purpose of God for us. A local church is in the will of God only as it is preoccupied with the planting of other local churches, at home and abroad. However independent the little body of believers may be, it has not attained God's goal for it until it is concerned that there be other individual believers and other groups of believers in every part of the world.

Working Yourself Out of a Job

Related to this myth of independency is the one best expressed in that counsel so often given to new missionaries, "Your job is to work yourself out of a job!" We shall not overlook the element of truth in this statement, but we need to face the fact that it is such an inadequate declaration of God's purposes as to have great potential for harm.

Let us first recognize the element of truth here. A missionary who is doing the same thing for the **79** same people as twenty years ago may well ask himself what is wrong. He may need to be exhorted in terms of the counsel quoted above, although it may be too late for it to help him very much.

But whatever truth there is in this idea has been vitiated by overstatement and by unintelligent repetition. The result is that truth has once again become myth.

The idea that a missionary has to do a job and then disappear from the scene is a distortion. This is clearly seen when we take the following factors into consideration.

His job will certainly change with the passing of the years—and it should be his aim that it do so. But there is another sense in which he will never be out of a job—whether he stays in one place or moves frequently from one country to another. The truth is that the task of a church in any given location is never done. It should always be discovering new areas—geographic, social, economic—that need to be evangelized. As Beyerhaus and Lefever put it, "There cannot be any excess of missionary service if it really restricts itself to spreading the Word and 'seeketh not its own.' In fact, we hear very little today in church circles in Asia and Africa that suggests in any way that the young churches not only do not need, but also do not want, the fellowship and service of foreign missionaries who will serve in this spirit, enjoined on his followers by our Lord Himself."[4]

What these men have observed in Asia and Africa is at least equally true in Latin America, where the national churches themselves plead for more missionaries—provided those missionaries come in the right spirit and with an understanding of their new role. The missionary is a part not only of the sending church but also of the church to which he has been sent, and as a member of the latter group he must have his eyes constantly open to new ways in which the people whom he serves can do their work for Christ, with him as their helper.

His relationship to this young church is in some ways more basic than his relationship to the church he has left behind. In many instances, God does not intend him to be a temporary factor on the scene. His role may change and his particular assignment may vary, but he will often fulfill the will of God only by refusing to disappear.

Of course, in some cases it may be better for him to go elsewhere; his personality and his attitudes may be such that the church will never develop fully while he is still on hand. (And in some few cases, it might have been better had he never come in the first place!) But the true servant of God, even though he comes from an alien culture, may become so identified with the church of his adoption that he will have a lifelong ministry in its midst. In such a case, the well-being of the local church will not necessarily demand his departure to other fields.

If a missionary comes to the church as a servant rather than as a master, and if he sees himself as a member of the order of the towel, that group of self-forgetting servants who find their inspiration in the foot-washing scene in the Upper Room, there are no limits to the contribution he can make to the church in the land of his adoption. In one sense, he will always be a foreigner there; in another sense no man is a foreigner in the body of Christ. Each group of believers is meant to be a place where God demonstrates the unity which his Spirit can bring to very diverse elements. The Lord wants to show how he can bring together those of widely differing backgrounds, enabling them to minister to one another and then to the world for which his Son died.

Working oneself out of a job is legitimate when it involves a readiness to cede authority and responsibility to capable nationals; it is a misstatement of biblical truth and consequently a myth when it is formalized into a general principle which demands that a missionary forever consider himself a temporary element on the scene.

Scaffolding

Again, the idea has been expressed in another way. We have frequently been told that missions are the scaffolding—an essential but temporary feature of a construction program. This emphasis has been healthy to the extent that it has reminded us that missionary effort is not an end in itself. When the "scaffolding" figure is a corrective in this regard, it is a worthy sort of emphasis. When it goes beyond this, as it usually does, and pictures missions as just one stage in the development of a church, it falls far short of the biblical picture and enters the realm of myth.

At that stage it becomes a dangerous thing because of the false concept it gives of the church of Christ and the limited understanding it shows of the missionary enterprise, which is inaccurately represented when it is likened to the scaffolding of a building.

Like many analogies, this one has been pushed too far. In the biblical picture, missions are not an appendage to be disposed of once the building is up, but an integral part of the structure. In this sense, every church is meant to be both a receiving and a sending group. To change the figure, missions are not a preliminary stage to church life but a continuing aspect of every healthy church, and the contribution of the missionary has not been fully made when a new church has been brought into being, or even, as we have seen, when it reaches a particular stage of independence.

This does not mean that the missionary has to mother the new group forever, or hover over it for a long period of time. Neither does it mean, however, that he is only an incident in its life. We have been in danger of repeating abroad the mistake we have made at home of presenting missions as a chapter in the life of the church—a beginning chapter or an epilogue—whereas the scriptural norm is that of a body of believers made up of many different backgrounds, personalities and cultures, but united in love for Christ and in a constant and continuing determination to make his love known to others, to the end that they, too, may be saved and banded together in churches.

Some missionary strategists, mistakenly I believe, have so uncritically accepted the "scaf- **83** folding" concept that they argue earnestly for an absolute and permanent separation between mission and church. Their arguments are not to be dismissed lightly, but it seems apparent that, by insisting on such a dichotomy, they not only are perpetuating the idea of missions as one stage in the church's life but also are seeing it as only one limited aspect of its work. Whatever limitations there may be to the ecumenical movement's insistence that "the church is mission," there is a great spiritual truth expressed in this phrase—a truth which in our evangelical camp we have often lost sight of, to our own detriment and to the detriment of missionary work around the world.

Paul Rees puts it well: "Some form of parallelism [between mission and church] may serve as a temporary measure, but it is not the wave of the future. It is the gurgle of the past. Neither continuing parallelism nor planned withdrawal is what Asian and African Christians want from the missionaries. They want integration, membership, the kind of mutual commitment that makes of twain one."[5]

In like fashion, Beyerhaus and Lefever quote representatives of the newer churches as saying at the Willengen Meeting in 1952, "We should cease to speak of Missions and Churches and avoid this dichotomy not only in our thinking but also in our actions. We should now speak of the mission of the church." Commenting further on this, Beyerhaus and Lefever write, "The ultimate aim of missions is no longer the organizational independence of the young church: it is rather the building up of a church which has itself a missionary outreach.''[6]

We have often so thoroughly embraced the scaffolding concept that we have misunderstood the purpose of God and our own role as Christians in it. And so we speak of ''churchmen'' and of ''missionaries'' as though these two groups had to be separate and distinct and were necessarily antithetical, and as though such a dichotomy had to be permanently maintained. Our thinking must be corrected at this point.

The biblical concept of missions must be understood and implemented by all of God's people—clergymen, missionaries, laity. It is God's purpose that his redeemed children should not only enjoy the blessings of salvation, but that they should also know the privileges and the responsibilities of discipleship. Our Lord's disciples came from diverse backgrounds and had varying gifts, but *all* of them were expected to go into the world and to preach the gospel as they went (Mt. 28:19-20). The members of the group who saw his ascension were *all* commissioned, without exception, to be his witnesses (Acts 1:8). The Scriptures never settle merely for the enjoyment of salvation by the people of God. The Lord bestows one or more gifts on each of his children, and he expects them to use them—for his glory and for the building up of the body of Christ (1 Pet. 4:10; Rom. 12:6-9). We have reason to believe that the Lord is delighted when people become members of his family through faith in his Son, but that he cannot be content until they share his missionary passion.

In the light of the New Testament, we, his ser- **85**

vants, know ourselves to be not merely the scaffolding but a part of the building itself, framed together for the honor and glory of Christ. Our trouble has been caused by goals that were too limited, if truly biblical standards for the church are to be accepted. We have thus accepted a myth and perpetuated it.

THE MYTH
OF THE UNQUALIFIED
NATIONAL

Not long ago a missionary executive expressed interest in the radical restructuring we had been doing in the Latin America Mission.[1] He asked me many perceptive questions about our efforts to root the work more thoroughly in Latin America and to make sure that it was Latin in its leadership and sense of direction. He wanted to know what hope we had of developing a true partnership between Latin Americans and North Americans—where we "foreign missionaries" would be the junior partners.

When I finished answering his questions, he said rather wistfully, "That's wonderful! I wish we could do the same thing in the country where we work. The only trouble is that the national Christians there aren't yet ready for such a step."

In replying to him, I wanted to be sympathetic and understanding of his position. Yet I felt that a word of warning was called for, too. I acknowledged that, since he knew the land of his adoption much better than I did, he would be a more capable judge than I. I was in no position to argue with his basic thesis. But I was afraid that he was in danger of perpetuating a myth.

I therefore told him that, if there were indeed valid grounds for his statement now, he would need to be careful that he was not saying the same thing five years from now, or ten years from now—because by then there would be no one to say it to!

I meant, of course, that if he postponed too long his readiness to trust the Holy Spirit's working in the national leadership of the church, he might well forfeit all opportunities of further usefulness in that church, in which he evidently had such limited confidence.

Not many mission leaders are as outspoken as he was. The myth of the unqualified national is not usually expressed so forthrightly; instead, it is implied by a host of things we say and do which indicate that we are not yet ready to trust the leadership God has raised up for his church in these countries.

Most of us missionaries would pay glowing tribute to the maturing church in the lands where we have served and to the emergence of a true national leadership in it. Often, however, our actions belie our words. It is all too evident that we feel that for some time to come we shall have to hang on tightly to the reins of authority. Meanwhile, we grudgingly give in here and there by delegating some reponsibility in less important areas, but seldom surrender major elements of the work into their hands unless we are forced to do it.

"But Not Now"

We are constantly in danger of underrating those whom God is raising up to lead his church. We are in similar danger of overrating our own importance. And so, like Augustine in his unconverted days, praying, "Lord, give me purity—but not now," we want to postpone any radical changes to the distant future.

The myth that we are considering here pays lip service to the national church and to its leadership. It glowingly describes the progress of that church and then, with a patronizing air which is not recognized by the one who adopts it, the real verdict is expressed: "They are not ready for the major role of leadership yet. We had better hold on to things in the meanwhile. Someday they will be ready, but not now." If I had asked the man who told me the nationals were not ready for leadership why he felt that way, he might well have related a series of stories of nationals, promoted to higher positions in the work of the church, who had miserably failed. (But of course he would not be likely to mention the long, sad record of *missionary* failures!)

He probably would have reminded me of how slow some of these young Christians are to be concerned about things that seem important to us, such as statistics, financial accounting, parliamen- **89** tary procedure, punctuality (as though, because *we* make much of these things in our culture, they must be equally important to God and should be to all his children!).

He might have gone on to tell me of some nationals he has known who do not want authority and responsibility (as though their attitude represented a fair cross section of the national church; this kind of faulty generalization reminds me of the man who was quoted as saying, "All Indians walk in single file; at least the one I saw did"!).

Underrated Potential

There will probably always be those who insist that the nationals are not ready, when in fact it is the missionaries' own unreadiness to cede power and authority which is the real obstacle. In most parts of the world, we missionaries have badly underrated the potential of the national leadership. We say they are not yet ready. Surely this is one of the most dangerous of the myths about missions.

The falsity of this particular position ought to be exposed, for at least five reasons:

1. *This myth does not fit the evidence.* In the commercial world, North American corporations have long since learned that their work on foreign soil is carried on best by those who are native to the culture. Sears, Roebuck & Co., for example, with a thriving business in Latin America, boasts that well over ninety percent of its staff there (including those in top-level positions) are Latin Americans. This policy not only makes the North

American company less vulnerable to expropriation; it means that the advance of the company into new areas is in the hands of those who know those areas best. Why have missions been so slow to adopt a similar policy?

One of the thrilling developments in the church in Latin America in recent years has been the emergence of a level of national leadership that would do credit to the Christian church in any land and that compares favorably with the best we have to offer in the States. I have been deeply impressed by the character and the gifts of the men whom God has brought to places of leadership in his church in Latin America. My life has been enriched, and the church of Christ has been wonderfully blessed, by the leadership of such men as Dr. Benjamin Moraes, outstanding lawyer, university professor and Presbyterian lay pastor of Brazil; Licenciado Ruben Lores, Cuban-born educator, leader in evangelism and rector of the Seminario Bíblico Latinoamericano in Costa Rica; Dr. Samuel Escobar, dynamic young intellectual of Peru, currently heading up the Inter-Varsity Christian Fellowship of Canada; and Dr. George Taylor, Panamanian psychologist, actively engaged in the training of young people for the service of Christ.

Here I mention only a few of the choice leaders God has given to his church in recent years in one of the so-called "mission fields." This list could be indefinitely lengthened.

2. *This myth glaringly reflects the vestiges of paternalism.* Most of us like to feel that we have been delivered from some of the attitudes which **91**

once characterized missions, but our slowness to cede authority and our failure to recognize and honor competent national leadership clearly testify that we have not yet been fully set free from the curse of paternalism.

Too often we are like well-meaning parents who keep postponing the time when they will let their children make their own decisions, and who deceive themselves into believing that their unwillingness to let go is dictated by love, when in reality they are dominated by a shallow sentimentality which is a miserable counterfeit of love.

We can always rationalize our failures in this area, dressing them up in pious expressions of concern for the future of the church or in glowing declarations of love for the people in it. But the truth is that our concern is often for our own status. And a love which does not include confidence is a poor imitation of the real thing. The trouble, many times, is not that our national brethren are unready for leadership but that we are too possessive and paternalistic to let them have it.

3. *This myth limits the potential of the national church and of its leadership.* While no one wants to see the church make unnecessary and costly mistakes, we need to remember that the possibility of making them is a part of the learning process, and that we do our brethren no favor by forever trying to guard them against that possibility. When we are honest with ourselves, we know that we have made our own best progress, both intellectually and spiritually, not when we were kept from decision-making with all its potential for wrong

choices, but when we were granted a measure of freedom that carried with it a possibility for evil as well as good.

This is the way God treated our first parents, and it is the way he deals with us. Dr. James Oliver Buswell, Jr., used to say that God could have made his creatures in the form of mechanical dolls who at the touch of a button would sing the Doxology. The Lord chose instead to let us be creatures with the ability to choose whether or not we would recognize his goodness to us. He thereby risked the possibility that we might choose wrongly. Only in this freedom would character and capacity for responsible action be possible.

There is always a sense in which experience is the best teacher, and we who have proven this in our own lives are culpable indeed if we try to deny others the opportunity of learning in this demanding school, even though it may on occasion be costly.

All of us have seen people who have forever had their decisions made for them, and who as a result are in their adult years still children—with tragic consequences. To repeat this kind of mistake in our dealings with national Christians is a blameworthy thing, one for which we shall have to give account to God.

There are many parts of the world today where the church of Christ would be more fully developed and mature if it had long since been given the right to make its own decisions, unpressured by well-meaning but oversolicitous foreign missionaries.

4. *This myth has been rejected by the national leadership* in most of the lands where we serve. Dennis Clark says that in many parts of the world the national Christian leaders have this as their target for the seventies: "To establish permanently and securely the principle that 'under God and led by His Spirit, we, His people, in this nation, will determine what is best for the evangelism of our people, and how most effectively to secure the development and strengthening of believers, so that they become fully involved as functioning members of Christ's Body.' "[2]

Too frequently, our spiritual sons and daughters see through the sham of our overprotectiveness and recognize that our slowness to give them their rightful place is not an evidence of love but a selfish desire for continuing power, inadequately covered over by pious cliches and manifestations of superficial sentimentality.

Another mission executive who talked with me about recent developments in the Latin America Mission commented, "I'm glad for what you are doing. We've done something like this on one of our fields recently, but unfortunately we were too slow in getting around to it, and we did it with a gun at our heads." He went on to describe the penalty they had paid for being tardy in granting to national leadership its rightful prerogatives.

His mission had prided itself on its Bible school in that particular country and had somehow convinced itself that the success of the school depended upon continued missionary leadership.
94 Eventually, rising up in open rebellion against this

attitude, national leaders announced that they were closing the school—by force—and that it would not reopen until the running of it was put into their hands. For a time a stalemate ensued, until mission leaders finally gave in and grudgingly turned over the reins.

I have no right to pass judgment on that situation nor on those concerned, but my missionary friend, who had been deeply involved, was not slow to do so. "It was our fault," he said. "We should have put the institute into their hands years ago. They saw through our slowness to let go and recognized our shortsighted lack of confidence in them. Had we been more prompt and more gracious, a crisis would have been avoided and a better fellowship would exist among us today."

Who can calculate the ultimate cost of such mistakes? Our love for the work of Christ will be measured not by overzealous guarding of our authority but by accepting what our national brethren have been saying to us: Missionaries can now serve the church best by acknowledging the gifts of the nationals and by granting them full authority in the church, while we gladly take a subordinate role in the work of Christ. Only the Lord can enable those of us who have been bosses to become servants, but he is able to do it and he longs to do it—now!

5. *This myth, if not dealt with promptly and effectively, will have violent repercussions in the work of Christ one of these days.* Like the Bible school mentioned above, many a missionary institution will come to the end of its usefulness, not because its work is really finished, but because

we missionaries have been so stubbornly insistent on having our own way. The patience of our national brethren will run out. When it does, the work of the church will suffer, but it will be our fault, not theirs. We can blame no one but ourselves for our slowness to read the signs of the times.

Rebellion

At one of the great congresses on evangelism in recent years, an explosive crisis arose because a North American group, which had invested heavily in the project, wanted something to say about the program. The national leadership saw this as a denial of their right and ability to plan their own meetings. They adamantly refused to agree to the request of the North Americans. The two sides were deadlocked, and the continuation of the congress itself was threatened.

Undoubtedly each of the two groups was somewhat at fault. But the real problem was in the seeming insistence of the North Americans that they knew best what should be on the program; it was a new expression of the myth that the people in these "mission fields" are not really ready to run their own affairs.

Fortunately, the North Americans gave in. But it was only the grace of God that prevented a disaster which would have had repercussions around the world and which might have reflected unworthily on the whole missionary enterprise.

If there are some places where the national leadership of the church is not yet ready to take over, there are hundreds of other places where they are ready but are denied the opportunity by well-meaning but shortsighted foreign missionaries. If we must err in this matter, let it be on the side of giving them authority and responsibility too quickly, rather than too slowly. The former error is in all likelihood much more forgivable and much less damaging than the latter.

Dennis Clark insists that the first goal of missions in the next decade must be "a final step in the transfer of all major policy-making concerning Christian ministry in the Third World to the nation and region concerned, in contrast to the present practice whereby many missionary organizations still plan and direct programs from their Western bases."[3]

Mr. Clark is right. We had better straighten out our thinking on this point, or we shall forfeit our right to continue to serve Christ in lands other than our own.

The myth of the unqualified national deserves to be seen for what it is—a false idea, prompted by well-meaning but unworthy motives, and capable of hurting terribly the work of Christ. If we are genuinely concerned for the welfare of the church, we shall pray and work for a partnership in which we missionaries shall serve under the choice indigenous leadership which God has raised up. That leadership is one of the great spiritual phenomena of our time.

8

THE MYTH
OF THE UNDERPAID
MISSIONARY

Almost every missionary conference I attend finds
the saints being called upon to sing, "So send I you,
to labor unrewarded; to serve unpaid, unloved, un-
sought, unknown." The congregation responds
heartily, putting the same fervor (and the same lack
of thought) into singing these words as they do into
harmonizing about Western empires who own
their Lord and savage tribes that attend his Word.

I have no idea what the average Christian is
thinking about when he sings such things, but I am
sure that both consciously and unconsciously he is
affected by his use of these words. The idea is
widespread in the evangelical churches of our land
that missionaries are poorly paid, neglected, forgotten, ignored—in effect utterly unrewarded, financially and in a dozen other ways.

In all fairness, it should be noted that there have been some grounds for believing these things. Missionaries are often put in a special category; we do not pay them on the same scale as we do our pastors. Some missionaries have been underpaid or not paid at all. It is not hard for a missionary to feel that he has been forgotten by those who promised so fervently to pray for him and to provide for his needs—sometimes that is true. It takes no great historical research to produce examples. The danger comes when we unwisely generalize on the basis of limited evidence.

This concept of missionary life does not come from Scripture, nor is it supported by any careful study of the experience of most missionaries. It is a myth, and should promptly be labeled as one.

Yet if it does not come from the Bible or from missionary experience, where does it come from? In part, it emerges from a form of evangelical hero worship, and since our "heroes" are not ordinarily noted for their affluence or for their fame, we try to make them noteworthy for their willingness to do without these two ingredients of worldly success.

Sometimes this myth of the underpaid missionary has its origin in a guilt complex which many of us feel. Since our own halfheartedness is roundly condemned by the obvious dedication of missionaries we have known, we feel obliged to render them tribute by insisting that, whatever their pay, they are worth a lot more than they get. Convicted that we have not done our part in praying or giving or going, we try to relieve our sense of guilt by making vows to do more, or we take the easier way out—by bestowing sympathy on the missionary. Somehow, such sympathy becomes a substitute for action; there is a certain virtue in feeling sorry for the underdog, whether or not you do anything for him. And if you can make his lot sound like a really difficult one, then your sympathy becomes even greater—and consequently more virtuous.

For these and other reasons, we have accepted an idea which both denies the truth of Scripture and contradicts the experience of a great host of God's choice missionary servants. The inevitable result has been myth—a myth which has had incalculable effects on the people of God and on their missionary outreach. It has perpetuated a concept of the missionary which is in reality a reflection on the One who sends him. And it has turned many promising candidates away in discouragement.

We have said that the myth of the underpaid missionary is a denial of Scripture. This could be proven from various parts of the Word of God, where we are reminded that God goes before and with his servants whom he sends out (Jn. 10:4); where we are assured that he will never forsake us (Heb. 13:5); where we are told that he notes and rewards every cup of cold water that we give in his name (Mt. 10:42); and where we learn that he is not forgetful of anything we do for him (Heb. 6:10).

Note especially Mark 10:29-30 where our Lord, in speaking to Peter, is not promising "pie in the sky by and by" but the rewards which his servant is to have here in this life, with persecutions: "Truly, I say to you, there is no one who has left house or brothers or sisters or mother or father or children or   **101** lands, for my sake and for the gospel, who will not receive a hundredfold now in this time, houses and brothers and sisters and mothers and children and lands, with persecutions, and in the age to come eternal life." I am not inclined to pass lightly over the prediction of persecution which is included here, but neither dare I overlook the assurance of our Lord that his servants will be amply rewarded here and now for anything they give up for his sake.

I was speaking about these verses in a church in New Jersey some years ago. Noting in the congregation two men from our Board of Trustees, I spontaneously found myself addressing them directly. One of them was the president of our board, and calling him by name I asked, "How many percent is 'a hundredfold'?" Smiling at my mathematical naivete, he replied, "That's easy—it's ten thousand percent!"

I turned to the other man, a Wall Street broker, and said, "Ray, suppose I had some money to invest. What stocks or bonds could you recommend that would pay me ten thousand percent?" He was as tolerant of my innocence as the other man had been of my ignorance, and he answered, "If I knew of stocks and bonds that would pay at that price, I'd have been a millionaire a long time ago. Wall Street doesn't pay that way!"

Of course it doesn't, but Jesus Christ, unless he be a liar, does. And if he does, then there is no such thing as an underpaid missionary. The very idea ought to be banished once and for all to the limbo of rejected myths. Moreover, in the light of this passage we scarcely dare speak of the "sacrifices" which a missionary makes. It would be more appropriate to speak of his "investments"!

No Rewards?

This myth is not only denied by Scripture; it is contradicted by the experience of a multitude of missionaries. I cite here three examples, fully confident that the stories of many others would likewise reinforce the conviction that no missionary is really underpaid.

One of my missionary colleagues was telling us recently of her joy in seeing what God had done in the lives of two young Costa Ricans. She had known both the boy and the girl from their childhood years—and had often had her heart broken as she endeavored to help them to know Christ, only to find them again and again rejecting the Savior. The girl in particular had not only been unresponsive; she had seemed utterly incorrigible. On many occasions the missionary, who was partially responsible for this child's upbringing, had felt the whole effort to be a total failure. The service of Christ, consequently, seemed unrewarding.

Her love was spurned, her kindness unappreciated. For years there was no response whatever on the part of these two, on whom the missionary had lavished such love and for whom she had prayed so much. It all seemed hopeless, and when the two married the situation looked no better.

For some time the missionary had no contact with the couple, but recently she met them again, unexpectedly, in the United States. She found them beautiful in their love for the Lord, for each **103** other and for the family God had given them. She discovered that they are actively serving Christ and wonderfully fruitful in that service.

The missionary suddenly saw herself richly repaid for all her prayers, her tears, her ostensibly unappreciated love. Looking back over her service for the Lord in Latin America, she said, "I wouldn't change my lot for that of anyone, anywhere. I have been bountifully rewarded for everything I've ever done for the Lord." Missionaries are underpaid? You would find her hard to convince!

Susan Strachan, co-founder of the mission which I serve, would never have swallowed this myth. She had left home, loved ones and a measure of ease and comfort for Christ's sake. But she lived to see the Lord give it all back to her a hundredfold: buildings wonderfully provided for the carrying on of his work; men, women and children won into the family of God and now her brothers and sisters in Christ; institutions raised up to speed his gospel to every part of Latin America. She now has her reward in heaven, but long before she went there she was paid, richly paid, here on earth—in a currency a millionaire might well envy.

The Really Important Thing

Missionaries are unknown? If you are talking about the headlines of the secular press, you are right. But my beloved friend and colleague, Ken Strachan, was to me all the evidence I shall ever need that God's servants are never really unknown—by him or by those who really matter here on earth. Ken never sought fame, and the secular world took little notice when God called him home a few years ago. Yet he was widely known and much loved throughout Latin America, especially by those who came to know Christ because Ken Strachan had led the Latin American church in the widest evangelistic outreach it had ever known.

I remember a Saturday morning in Caracas, Venezuela, when thousands of people were crammed together in a sports arena which had never known a gathering like it before. The throng had just come from a great parade through the city streets where they had borne witness to their new life in Christ. Now, in a tremendous evangelistic rally, they were marking the conclusion of a yearlong effort, known as Evangelism-in-Depth, to get the gospel of Christ to every person in Venezuela.

The mood was one of rejoicing and of great thanksgiving for what God had done. In the midst of the service, the national chairman reminded the assembled crowd that the man whom God had used to bring Evangelism-in-Depth into being, Kenneth Strachan, was near death in a Pasadena, California, hospital. He suggested that all join together in prayer for Dr. Strachan.

I've never heard anything like it. Seven thousand people, all praying aloud at the same time, their voices surging and receding like great waves of the sea, giving thanks for a servant of God who had blessed their lives and committing him to the Lord's gracious keeping. Suddenly, the world's headlines seemed very unimportant, the world's fame very transitory. It is nice to be known, but the really important thing, I saw that morning, is to be **105** known by God and by people who have been drawn to him through your faithful service. And I knew that in this sense the Lord's servants are never unknown and surely never underpaid.

So let this myth be recognized for what it is: a calumny against a faithful God and an appeal for sympathy that is neither needed nor wanted by the missionary. The Lord's servants may need support, but not pity. His is an honorable calling and a privileged one, and it ought to be presented as such.

9

MISSIONS WITHOUT MYTHS

The ideal of missions without myths is noble—noble, but seemingly impossible to attain. After all, any institution or movement tends to develop its own traditions—to gather around itself ideas and concepts which may or may not be in accord with its original purposes. Any living, growing movement needs to be constantly alert lest its basic message be corrupted, lest its motivations become less sound than they once were, lest its methods prove unworthy of its message.

These were some of the real dangers faced by the early Christian church. Myth often threatened to take over in place of truth. The believers soon found that they had to be forever on guard against false elements and emphases which easily could creep into the doctrine of the church. Paul's letter to the Galatians was a stern warning against this possibility and a call to vigilance against it. It is all too easy for pretense to take the place of reality, as the Christians learned in the case of Ananias and Sapphira (Acts 5). The early believers were constantly in danger of accepting that which God had rejected (for example, the idea of righteousness by works of the law), or of rejecting that which God had accepted (for example, the "unclean" Gentiles in Acts 10). Had they not constantly been on the alert, myth, rather than God's truth, might well have been the distinguishing characteristic of the new movement.

From the beginning of the Christian church, there was always the possibility that it would settle for being something less than God meant it to be. The same danger haunts the missionary movement in our day, and in every day. The Christians of the first century discovered that their only protection against confusion as to message, motivations and methods was an awareness of the danger and a constant and continual submission of their thoughts to God's standard.

So it is with the missionary enterprise. We think we have slain the dragons of missionary mythology, only to discover that they refuse to stay dead or constantly reappear in new forms. Myths are inevitable in the realm of missions—unless we are aware of their danger and continually depend on the Lord to help us recognize and expose them.

The only corrective for falsehood is truth—God's truth. The only hope of having missions without myths lies in our readiness to bring all our beliefs, our attitudes, our thoughts under the judgment of God's Word. The ideal of missions without myths is impossible, in one sense; but then, so are all the ideals of the Christian life—utterly impossible of human attainment, except as the Spirit of God possesses us and enables us, in the strength of Christ, to do the impossible. He will enable us to distinguish between truth and myth and to think his thoughts, rather than our own, about the glorious privilege and awesome responsibility of making Christ known to all men everywhere.

Notes

Chapter 1

[1]Quoted by Gerald H. Anderson in *The Future of the Christian World Mission*, William J. Danker, ed. (Grand Rapids: Eerdmans, 1971), p. 139.

[2]Norman A. Horner, *Protestant Crosscurrents in Mission* (Nashville: Abingdon, 1968), p. 10.

[3]F. Dean Lueking, "The Local Church" in *The Future of the Christian World Mission,* p. 121.

Chapter 2

[1]Elton Trueblood, *The Validity of the Christian Mission* (New York: Harper & Row, 1972), p. 69.

[2]At the risk of inconsistency, the word "missionary" is occasionally used elsewhere in this book in the popularly accepted sense of one called by God to cross geographic, linguistic or cultural frontiers. But the basic emphasis of this chapter is that in the biblical perspective the term "missionary" ought to include anyone who at the call of God goes anywhere to make the gospel known.

[3]John Howard Yoder, *As You Go* (Scottsdale, Pa.: Herald Press, 1961).

[4]Trueblood, p. 71.

Chapter 4

[1]Burgess Carr, "Controversy Surrounds Missionaries" (United Press International, Nairobi), *Paterson News*, February 12, 1973, p. 5.

Chapter 5

[1]Prudencio Damboriena, "Aspects of the Missionary Crisis in Roman Catholicism," in *The Future of the Christian World Mission*, p. 73.

[2]Ibid., p. 76.

[3]Arthur Glasser, "Theology: with or without the Bible," *Church Growth Bulletin* (January, 1971), III, 112-14, quoting Donald Dawe in *The Future of the Christian World Mission*, p. 64.

[4]Harold Lindsell, "The Evangelical Missions: the Home Base," *The Future of the Christian World Mission*, p. 95.

[5]John Howard Yoder, the Mennonite theologian, has written a helpful booklet, entitled *As You Go*. His thesis is that, in the original Greek of the Great Commission, the imperative is "to preach" and "to make disciples," not "to go into all the world." This latter phrase, he points out, is not a command but a qualifying idea, with the result that the Great Commission might better be translated, "As you go into all the world, preach the gospel...."

Chapter 6

[1]Beyerhaus and Lefever, *The Responsible Church and the Foreign Mission* (Grand Rapids: Eerdmans, 1964), p. 16.

[2]Ibid., p. 12.

[3]C. Peter Wagner, *Frontiers in Missionary Strategy* (Chicago: Moody, 1972), pp. 166-67.

[4]Beyerhaus and Lefever, pp. 173-74.

[5]Paul Rees, editorial, *World Vision Magazine* (March, 1969).

[6]Beyerhaus and Lefever, p. 167.

Chapter 7

[1]For a fuller presentation of what was involved in this re-structuring of a mission, see the author's chapter, "Latin-americanizing the Latin America Mission," in the symposium, *Church-Mission Tensions Today*, C. Peter Wagner, ed. (Chicago: Moody, 1972).

[2]Dennis E. Clark, *Missions in the Seventies* (Scripture Union, 1970), p. 94.

[3]Ibid., p. 33.